TERESA'S REFLECTIONS - I

VENEZUELA, THE POPE, AND MORE

TERESA DI SCLAFANI DE NASCA

TecnoTur
Publishing
Is there a book inside you?

CONTENTS

Teresa's Reflections - I

Venezuela, the Pope, and more

Published by TecnoTurPublishing.com

Layout by Allan Tépper

ISBN of the paperback:

979-8-9934183-0-8

ISBN of the ebook:

979-8-9934183-1-5

I dedicate this work to:

- My son, Professor Carlos Sayas Torres, who was born a miracle. A hug and kiss from your mother who loves you so much.
- My sons Toni and Enzo.
- My three grandchildren, Salvatore Jesús, Enzito, and Salvatore Antonio.

Kisses to all…

CONTEMPORARY HISTORY OF VENEZUELA

CHAPTER 1
CONTEMPORARY HISTORY OF VENEZUELA

The great fighter María Corina Machado will go down in history. She is the granddaughter of Mr. Machado, an entrepreneur and hard worker who discovered that pig fat could be used to make lard under the brand *Los Tres Cochinitos* (which in English means: «the three little pigs»). This strong-willed and very humane man, who was always concerned about the poor, to whom he gave his lard, built a large company. María Corina's parents also inherited the company *Los Tres Cochinitos*, as it was formerly known, and now it is sold in every country at a low price, within everyone's reach.

We are talking about the courageous Corina, married and mother of two boys, who chose to send them with her husband outside of Venezuela to have a better life and security. She studied industrial engineering and sacrificed herself for her country. When she saw that her courageous policies were overcoming barriers, she prepared to continue her political struggle for Venezuela.

Since Chávez came to power in 1989, there have been many years of endurance. Chávez was not apparently bad, but he mortgaged the country until 2030, and it is not known until when, because not a single cent has been paid yet. Seeing the impossibility of staying in Venezuela, he fled to Cuba. The facts: Chávez staged a coup with several military officers, but it failed. However, Caracas suffered the disasters of war. In Maracaibo, there was a cardinal who remained in the government because Chávez returned.

Mr. Caldera, as president, was his godfather. He did not censure him even though he had staged a coup and belonged to the Sao Paulo Forum, which everyone knew. But Venezuelans, tired of cheap politics, believed him to be the next General Pérez Jiménez. They voted for him, and Fidel Castro helped him take control of Venezuela until it suited him, as he gave him oil and money. When Chávez stopped sending him oil and money, there was Mr. Maduro, of Colombian origin and educated in Cuba. It suited them better in the long run.

. . .

Chávez, seeing that Fidel apparently loved him, went to Cuba and left Maduro behind. Fidel took it upon himself to fix Chávez to his liking, and so, after a long time, Mr. Chávez returned, only to die shortly thereafter. He was unrecognizable, fat, and swollen, as seen on television. Everyone wondered what happened to Chávez in Cuba, and to this day it remains a mystery.

Since the Chávez era, Corina has been fighting, first against Chávez and then against Maduro, who is worse than Chávez. She has been threatened and nearly killed on several occasions. She has been ambushed, but God has always saved her. It is impossible to campaign, but Corina always rides on top of trucks during her very dangerous campaigns, even though they block the road to prevent her from reaching her destination. But Corina's politics reach every corner of Venezuela.

Mr. Cabello disqualified her from running for president for 15 years, but Corina continues to fight for Venezuela, without fear, looking for new people to be presidents. Unfortunately, everyone is afraid of Mr. Maduro, but at the last minute, on July 28, Mr. González, who has extensive experience working in various embassies during Mr. Chávez's term, was found. They could not disqualify him because they did not have time, that was the reality, but unfortunately, he still does not hold the Presidency of the Bolivarian Republic of Venezuela.

· · ·

González is well accepted as president in all countries except communist countries. That is why he is in exile in Spain with the consent of the Spanish president. He is a highly respected man, along with his entire family. What will happen to him? We will see what the future holds.

What happened ? She is in the Argentine embassy, cared for by Brazil. They cut off their electricity at any moment, leaving them with candles. They cut back on Corina Machado's daily meals so as not to run out of food, because there are six people accompanying her, but she is safe until Mr. Maduro leaves. We still don't know when that will be; it could be years, months, or days. That has been the fate of this great woman named Corina Machado, the woman of the year who is making a name for herself in the world. From here in the United States of America, I say to her, «Hang in there, Corina. What's coming is for the best.»

POPE FRANCIS AND VENEZUELA

CHAPTER 2
POPE FRANCIS AND VENEZUELA

In Venezuela, everyone is united in one voice, calling on Pope Francis, who has not remembered the Venezuelans, nor the Cubans, nor the Nicaraguans. He only thinks about communism, and I say that is what brings ill-gotten money to the Vatican. He always asked Cubans for patience, while he embraced the Castros. He has never had a word for Venezuelans or Cubans. Nor a word for Machado, who is a great woman of struggle, or for the prisoners who are beaten with stones.

This is the true face of Pope Francis: not asking forgiveness for so many cardinals violating the rules. In Canada, next to the convent, there are 4,200 young people who were raped, and no one has asked for forgiveness. I, Teresa Di Sclafani De Nasca, am saying this with great authority. I knew Pope John

XXIII, who was very good, and Pope John Paul II. He came twice to Venezuela, to the state of Portuguesa, and the people could not fit in the state.

Elections were held on July 28, 2024, and Mr. González is still not president; he is in exile in Spain. He never said anything, but he embraced Chávez and Maduro.

When Pope John XXIII died, they put in a Pope who lasted 24 years. Now someone is knocking on their doors with a cup in their hands. That Pope was dead, and no one knew what happened. A hundred years ago, a pope excommunicated the Freemasons, and the Freemasons overthrew that pope. Another pope came along and lifted the excommunication. I'm not just saying this; it's in a book.

MY GREAT-GRANDFATHER

_____

_____

_____

_____

_____

_____

_____

_____

_____

_____

_____

CHAPTER 3
MY GREAT-GRANDFATHER

My great-grandfather Lucio Orfanello studied to be a priest, but after completing his advanced studies, he took off his cassock. This can be verified and took place in Cefalù, Palermo, Sicily, Italy. He worked for 40 years at the post office as a telegraph operator and at the bank. He slept at the post office during World War I. Families told him he was waiting for news about their children.

He died before I could walk. After he died, I went to say goodbye to his daughter Ignacia, here in the United States.

He married and had four daughters and two sons, one of whom died. One of those daughters was my grandmother, who was born in 1890 and died in 1972. My mother always told me that my grandfather used to say to them, «Go to Mass and don't go into the sacristy.»

I met Father Sagona in my village of Alia in Palermo, Italy, Sicily. He was a priest and his brother was a mafioso. The latter raped a 16-year-old girl. They hid the affair and she had a son who became a priest, Father Gibino, who married me in 1959. They hid the family and took them to the countryside, making it seem as if the child had been born to the sister and her husband. But the whole village knew because they brought in a midwife named Doña Agustina, and she didn't hide it from anyone; she talked about it as if it were normal.

I met her when I was 11 years old, when I went to learn how to embroider. Mrs. Manina was next door, and she wants what happens in the Church. No one can hide the problems of the Church; it's not her fault.

THE MIRACLES I RECEIVED

_____

_____

_____

_____

_____

_____

_____

_____

_____

_____

_____

CHAPTER 4
THE MIRACLES I RECEIVED

I have received seven miracles in total. I even have a son, a great cardiologist, who was born from a miracle. He appeared to me twice at the Caracas airport. He had already graduated, as recorded in my diary on pages 43 and 44.

Fifty-seven years ago, my youngest son was one year old and had a fever that would not go down no matter what we did. At midnight, he died. I was 27 years old, with a dead child in my arms. I invoked Doctor José Gregorio Hernández, and after half an hour, he came back to life. We went to the Calicanto Clinic because we lived in Maracay. He had a fever of 105 degrees, and they put him in a bathtub filled with water and ice. The next day, he had sores in his mouth. My son Toni was 7 years old, and his cousin was 8.

. . .

With my two sisters-in-law who live in Maracay and are still alive, we took a plaque to the place where he was born and another to Caracas, where Doctor José Gregorio Hernández is buried. Later, the witch doctors worked with his spirit, and the Pope did not recognize his miracles. In 2021, a young woman had an accident and developed a tumor in her head, and he cured her. Seeing this, the Pope made him Blessed José Gregorio Hernández.

In my village, Alia di Palermo, Sicily, Italy, I made the saint, and he was presented on June 18, 2023, by Antonio Vicari, the parish priest.

On December 23, I had a day of feasting, and on the afternoon of the 24th, we had to go to my husband's family home. It turns out that we grabbed our suitcases from the hallway and forgot about the food. A hundred kilometers away, I remembered the food and said to my husband, «What do you want to do?» He said, «I'm going to call Mr. Idalgo.» He told him that we had forgotten the food and that he should eat it himself.

On the way back, the lawyer and theologian Gastón Saldivia said to me, «You didn't forget it; it was God who made you forget it. He's not working, and neither is his wife.» He had even made a promise to walk to Caracas, a 350-kilometer walk. He tells his neighbors that he came with his feet bleeding.

In 1994, Caldera became president and appointed him Director of Sports. His first trip was to Perú. There was a company that made Nasca t-shirts, and he brought me one. He came up to me and said, «I brought you a small gift.» I replied, «It's very important to me, and I'll keep it as a souvenir.»

In another miracle, we met Monsignor Juan Portuchese, who had spent many years in Poland with Pope John Paul II, who at that time was not yet Pope. He came to Barquisimeto, Venezuela, and built the Church of Fátima, which is very beautiful. We lived nearby in 1999 and were having some problems at work because people weren't paying their bills. I said to my husband, «Let's go pray the Rosary with Monsignor.» That day we were alone, but later the field filled up. My husband wasn't fond of Mass, but since he met Monsignor, he never missed Mass on Sundays.

His right arm was holy and he healed many people. There was Mrs. Asunción, a Portuguese woman whom I had known for 40 years. She always arrived before me. When I arrived, I would say to her, «Asunción, get up. This seat belongs to Doña Teresa.»

OUR OFFICE IN ORLANDO

———

———

———

———

———

———

———

———

———

———

———

CHAPTER 5
OUR OFFICE IN ORLANDO

My son was already in the spare parts business in Orlando and told his dad that he didn't have time to import. At that time, imports had to go through the port of Miami, and the company had only one distributor, Requieca. My husband wanted to sell the business to my son Enzo. I told them, «The business is not for sale. I'm going to Miami.» I bought the ticket, but on Sunday, when I was about to leave, I had severe back pain. I told my husband, «Let's go to Monsignor's.» He relieved my back pain, then patted me on the back and said, «Doña Teresa, go, everything will be fine.»

I got out of the car at the first hotel I saw. At that time, it cost US$130, and I couldn't afford it. I looked in the phone book and saw that Coral Gables was more central and cost US$60. I went straight to the hotel, and they gave me a very large room with a refrigerator, coffee maker, sandwich maker, a table, and two chairs. They would bring me the bill in the morning, and at night I could eat in my room. Three blocks away there was a store called Navarro, and at noon I could eat at the hotel restaurant, which was good.

I looked for a lawyer to set up the corporations, and when he did, he put their addresses on them. The problem was that the office had a «For Sale» sign. I walked down, called, and they closed. I got to the hotel and asked the owner, «Do you know where I can rent an office?» «I don't know,» he replied, but then he thought about it and took me to the manager. We agreed that there was a small space between the commercial premises and the hallway that cost US$1,800 for six months.

I paid him and went to buy a fax machine, a desk, and a chair. The fax machine was set up by the administrator, who had severe phlebitis in one leg. He set it up on the floor, and I started feeding sheets of paper through it. The company called me, saying that the sheets were duplicated and that couldn't see them properly. I went to the reception desk and there were two Peruvians who adjusted it for me. One of them is still there.

ON THE RADIO

____

____

____

____

____

____

____

____

____

____

____

ON THE RADIO

Teresa Di Sclafani De Nasca's books are featured on *CapicúaFM* radio, which can be heard across the globe on CapicúaFM via CapicúaFM.com and leading podcast apps.

ABOUT THE AUTHOR

———

———

———

———

———

———

———

———

———

———

ABOUT THE AUTHOR

Teresa Di Sclafani De Nasca was born in Italy. She has also lived in Venezuela and the United States.

OTHER WORKS BY
TERESA DI SCLAFANI DE NASCA

—————

—————

—————

—————

—————

—————

—————

—————

—————

—————

OTHER WORKS BY TERESA DI SCLAFANI DE NASCA

- *The world according to Teresa Di Sclafani*
- *The Diary of Teresa Di SclafaniThe Mafia according to Teresa Di Sclafani*
- *Nonna's Stories - I*
- *Nonna's Stories - II*

Each is available in Castilian, English and Italian.

www.ingramcontent.com/pod-product-compliance
Lightning Source LLC
Chambersburg PA
CBHW040905120626
46551CB00006B/661